Title: "Ida B. Wells-Barnett: A Journey of Courage and Forgiveness"
Author: Norma McLauchlin
Illustrated by: Jasmine Price

Ida B. Wells-Barnett
A Journey of Courage and Forgiveness

Ida B. Wells-Barnett was a fearless journalist and activist who fought for justice and equality. Her story is not just about her fight against injustice but also about the power of forgiveness.

Ida B. Wells was born on July 16, 1862, in Holly Springs, Mississippi. She was the daughter of enslaved parents and grew up in a world filled with challenges.

Despite the difficulties, Ida was determined to get an education. She attended Rust College and later became a teacher, believing education was key to empowerment.

Ida began writing about the injustices she witnessed. She used her pen to expose the harsh realities of racism and violence against African Americans.

After the lynching of her friend, Ida B. Wells decided to investigate and report on these tragic events. She was brave and unafraid to speak the truth.

Throughout her life, Ida faced tremendous anger and pain due to injustice. However, she understood that holding onto anger could not bring about real change. She chose to embrace forgiveness as a way to heal herself and her community.

11

Ida traveled across the country, giving speeches about her findings on lynching and advocating for civil rights. She encouraged people to unite for justice.

Ida B. Wells-Barnett co-founded the NAACP and continued to fight for women's rights and equality. Her courage inspired many to stand up against injustice.

Ida's legacy lives on. She inspires people today to fight for justice and to embrace forgiveness as a powerful tool for change.

Ida once said, 'The way to right wrongs is to turn the light of truth upon them.' Let's remember her words and continue to seek the truth.

Just like Ida, we can all make a difference. Whether it's standing up for a friend or learning about our history, we can create positive change together.

22

Ida knew that working together was essential for change. Let's build a community of kindness and forgiveness.

Acts of kindness and forgiveness can change lives. Let's remember Ida B. Wells-Barnett's example and treat everyone with respect and compassion.

Ida B. Wells-Barnett dreamed of a world where everyone was treated equally. Let's keep that dream alive by working together and forgiving one another.

28

Now it's your turn! How will you make a difference? Think about what you can do to help others and stand up for what is right.

Ida B. Wells-Barnett showed us that with courage, deteion, we can change the world. Forgiveness is a key part of that change.

Let's celebrate hope, kindness, and justice for everyone. Together, we can build a world where all are treated equally.

Ida B. Wells-Barnett's life was a journey of courage and forgiveness. She taught us that even in the face of hardship, we can choose to forgive and help others.

Ida B. Wells-Barnett's life was a journey of courage and forgiveness. She taught us that even in the face of hardship, we can choose to forgive and help others.

July History Highlights:

July 4, 1776 The Declaration of Independence is adopted in the United States, marking the birth of the nation and its ideals of freedom and equality.

July 16, 1862: Ida B. Wells-Barnett is born, destined to become a pioneering journalist and civil rights activist.

July 26, 1948: President Harry S. Truman signs Executive Order 9981, desegregating the armed forces, a significant step toward equality in the U.S. military.

July is a month that celebrates freedom and progress, reminding us of the ongoing journey toward justice and equality for all.

Additional titles in this series:

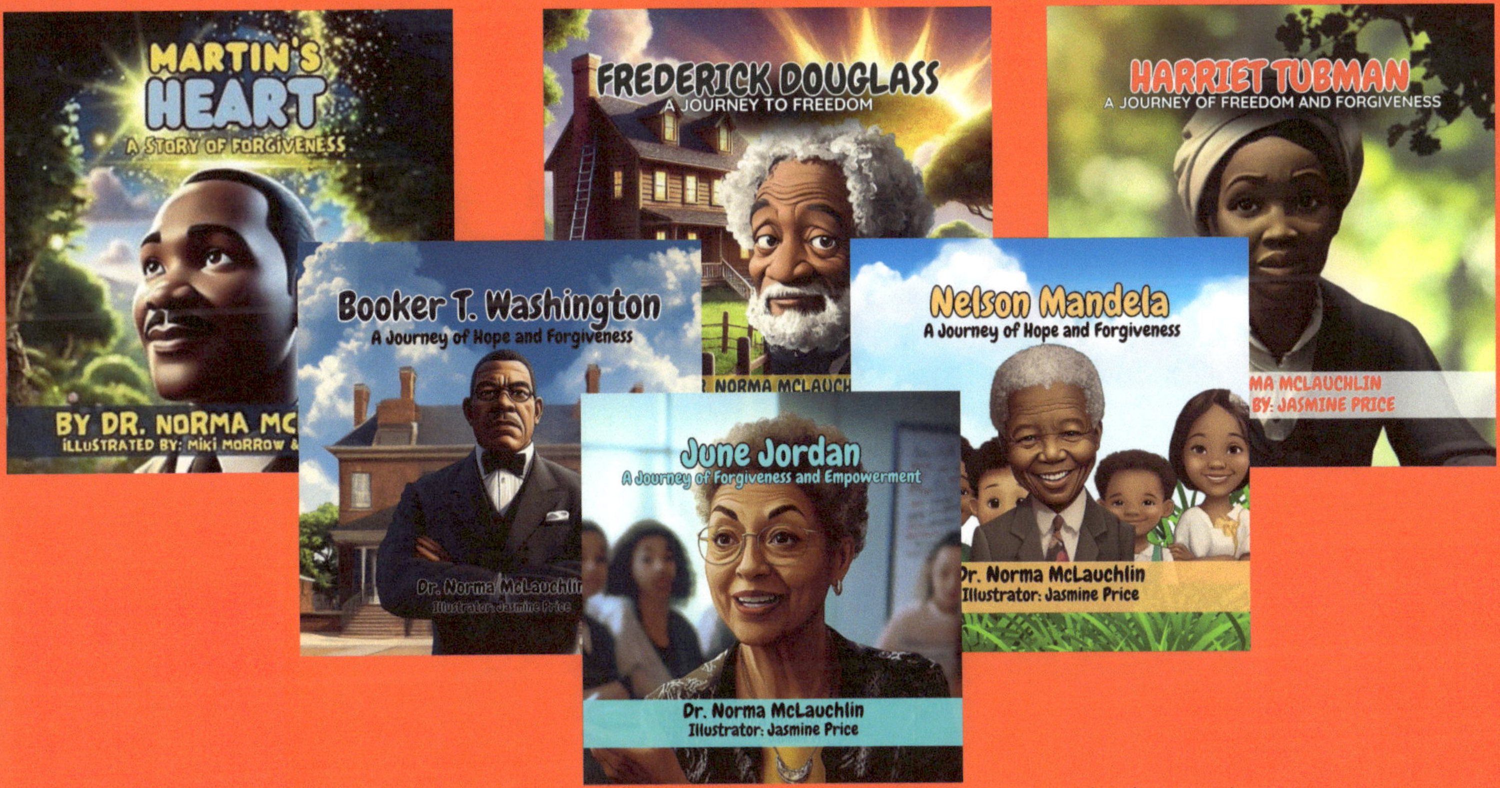

Look out for more exciting titles!